BOLD KID

Ancient China

RESCUE VEHICLE FACTS AND PICTURE BOOK FOR KIDS

If you're looking for some fascinating facts about Ancient China for kids, read on! The ancient Chinese civilization lasted more than 2,000 years. It was characterized by its diverse art, architecture, literature, and religious beliefs.

There were three major religions in ancient China: Buddhism, Taoism, and Confucianism. The culture's emphasis on nature and respect for the individual was reflected in its science, medicine, and technology.

The oldest civilization in the world, China has been inhabited for more than 4,000 years. Written records of the Chinese past date back to the Shang dynasty, which lasted from around 1600 BC to 1046 BC. Many Chinese cities have ancient ruins and were once the seat of royalty.

But it was the Xia dynasty (sh) that influenced the rest of the world. After the Shang era, the Zhou dynasty (Joe) dominated the region. The Shang emperor was the last period to be included in the Ancient era. The next two dynasties were called the Western Zhou and the Eastern and Final Zhou. The Imperial era followed this time frame.

While the Chinese culture was famous for its art and culture, there is plenty more to explore about this fascinating region. For instance, Chinese people invented the written language. Their alphabet had more than 80,000 characters, but it was shortened to just 40,000 to make it easier to read.

One of the most famous works of ancient Chinese literature is The Art of War, written by Sun Tzu during the Spring and Autumn Period. The text is more than 2500 years old and remains relevant today. Besides, ancient China is home to the Yangtze River and the Yellow River. Several mythical creatures, including dragons, were introduced to the country by Chinese authors.

The Chinese are among the oldest civilizations in the world. The Xia dynasty is considered the cradle of Chinese civilization. Other periods of ancient history include the Shang dynasty, the Zhou dynasty, and the Imperial era.

The ancient Chinese had the first written language in the world, and they were one of the first to do it. The Chinese also introduced many philosophical works.

The Chinese people were the first people to develop a written language. Although the alphabet was still not very complex, it was widely used in ancient times. For example, the earliest Chinese alphabet was more than 80,000 characters long, but the earliest writing was in poems.

Only affluent people could write poetry, so there were no aristocratic philosophers. The Chinese also developed a complex understanding of mathematics, astronomy, and mathematics.

The Chinese were the first people to develop a written language. The Chinese alphabet was composed of 40,000 characters. The Chinese were the first to develop a complex writing system. They also introduced Buddhism and were the only people in the world to have a written language.

The ancient Chinese were the first to develop the printing press. They were also among the first to introduce writing to the world. They also invented the wheel. There are many other interesting facts about Ancient China for kids, including the importance of the Great Wall.

The Chinese were one of the oldest civilizations in the world. They ruled their country for over 4,000 years. Some of them were brutal and cruel, but their culture was rich in inventions.

The Chinese emperors built a wall to protect their people from invasions. These are just a few of the many fascinating facts about Ancient China for kids! Just be sure to teach your children about this fascinating culture!

The Chinese emperors were the first rulers in the world. The emperor was known as a emperor. The emperor was also known as the "Dragon God" and was worshiped in the royal courts.

There are also many fascinating historical events about the ancient Chinese civilization. For example, the Buddhist calendar dates back more than 2,500 years. This is one of the oldest civilizations in the world.

Lightning Source UK Ltd.
Milton Keynes UK
UKHW050743140223
416940UK00010B/141